Facing Death

Facing Death

Rachel Boulding

The Bible Reading Fellowship
15 The Chambers, Vineyard
Abingdon OX14 3FE
brf.org.uk

The Bible Reading Fellowship (BRF) is a Registered Charity

ISBN 978 0 85746 564 1
First published 2017
10 9 8 7 6 5 4 3 2 1
All rights reserved

Acknowledgements
Scripture quotations from The New Revised Standard Version of the Bible, Anglicised Edition, copyright
© 1989, 1995 by the Division of Christian Education of the National Council of the Churches of Christ in
the United States of America, are used by permission. All rights reserved.

Extracts from the Authorised Version of the Bible (The King James Bible), the rights in which are vested
in the Crown, are reproduced by permission of the Crown's Patentee, Cambridge University Press.

Scripture quotations from The Holy Bible, New International Version (Anglicised edition) copyright
© 1973, 1978, 1984, 2011 by Biblica, are used by permission of Hodder & Stoughton Publishers,
an Hachette UK company. All rights reserved. 'NIV' is a registered trade mark of Biblica (formerly
International Bible Society). UK trademark number 1448790.

Extracts from The Book of Common Prayer of 1662, the rights of which are vested in the Crown in
perpetuity within the United Kingdom, are reproduced by permission of Cambridge University Press,
Her Majesty's Printers.

A catalogue record for this book is available from the British Library

Printed and bound by Rainbow Print

Foreword

As a priest, I have encountered death many times: in dimly lit hospital wards; in the ravaged faces of parents mourning the loss of a child; in the shock of diagnosis and the subsequent maze of consultations and operations, with its dead ends and dizzying turns... the place is reached where a person can no longer be accompanied and must travel on alone.

Every death is unique, every journey towards it an individual exploration of the light and dark that make up our lives, but they all bear resemblances to each other, which it can be helpful to discover and identify. Rachel Boulding's reflections on her journey spring from her personal situation, but they have relevance to us all, as she shares with us her struggles—the challenge of processing the diagnosis and the complexity of medical terminology, the tragedy of witnessing its effect on those who love her, the potentially terrifying nature of the end time.

Rachel gives us words to say when we wish to draw back and say nothing, and she shows how to offer our support to those we love. More precious, however, are the wonderful glimpses she gives us of the faith that sustains her in the most difficult of times. We marvel at her courage as she gives thanks for her awareness of her situation, which gives her time to prepare herself and those she loves. And above all, we can learn from her example, making the most of the opportunities that are offered to us and determining to experience God's redemptive love as fully as possible, sharing it with others and reminding ourselves daily of his grace. Let us, like Rachel, be prepared to accept the dangers and delights of the journey, open to every day's adventure.

As we, in our turn, grow near the end of our earthly pilgrimage, let us hope that we face it with the courage and hope that Rachel shows in these reflections. Let us trust also in the assurance of a constant travelling companion, who not only walks alongside us, but comes to meet us, as we approach our journey's end, ready to embrace us and lead us home: 'And if I go and prepare a place for you, I will come back and take you to be with me that you also may be where I am' (John 14:3, NIV).

Sally Welch, editor of *New Daylight* Bible reading notes

Introduction

When I suggested writing something about my situation of having terminal cancer, the kind editors at BRF encouraged me, saying that it would be useful to hear from someone going through the middle of a particular experience—rather than having what others might think about it from the outside. So many of us Christians are so eager to chip in with ideas about what others ought to be doing or feeling, or what we think the Bible says about a subject, that sometimes the heart of what it feels like gets lost. There can be something valuable in hearing about the experience from the inside, right now as it is happening.

Often, big events in life, such as bereavement or serious illness, are hard to imagine beforehand. They can feel very different from what we had expected, as well as being varied in people's varied circumstances. So I have tried to be as honest as I can, even when it involves bewilderment and uncertainty.

For some people, I realise, these big experiences lead to serious questioning of their beliefs or even a loss of faith. While I would always try to respect what they are going through, that has not been the case for me. Through no effort or merit of my own, I have found this to be an oddly unexpected time of blessing. Perhaps I am being naive, but I really am trying to be true to what is happening and how it has struck me, not just write what decent Christians might expect or wish to hear.

So I have tried to go through some of the various aspects of facing a life-limiting illness, as they have occurred to me, in terms of what such things can mean, both for the person who is dying and for those around him or her. This is not a linear progression with tightly defined stages, but a matter of varied facets coming into view at particular times, then fading away, only to return—often in a slightly different way. In some respects, this is similar to the experience of bereavement.

Most of the material in this booklet began life as daily Bible-reading notes, which explains the format of reflections on a passage, with a tight word-count to fit on to a single page. I could have bored on at greater length. But, of course, you don't need to stick to reading one page a day, and you can go through the pieces in as many sittings as you like. The separate pages of Bible verses and prayers are designed for reflection; they can form opportunities to pause and ponder what you make of what you are reading.

These are only short reflections. I feel as if I am barely scratching the surface of the subject. But whatever you think about death, I hope that you will feel encouraged to talk about it with those closest to you. This will be uncomfortable, but even a quick word about your hopes, plans and fears might be able to reassure them, and help lay to rest some anxieties. So many people have said to me, heavy with regret: 'We never had that conversation. I'll never know what he really thought.' You might have a chance to help lift such burdens, from yourself and others.

In what I have written, I have tried to frame everything in the context of all life being a gift from God, to be celebrated in the light of his love for each of us. Our purpose on this earth is to love, and to reflect God's amazing lovingkindness among others, within ourselves, and with God himself. He first loved us, and he lives in us now; it is he who works deep within us, not any feeble efforts of our own. We have our being in him, delighting in his wonderful grace.

This means that we can trust God with our future. Whatever lies before us, we can be assured of his care. All of us have natural human fears about dying, but there is a sense in which we really need not be afraid. God has given doctors skill in healing, so that they can allieviate much of our physical pain, and hospices—many of them, as with the whole modern hospice movement, founded by Christians—can offer great comfort. Whatever we think about our future life, we are going to be with God, in his nearer presence. He loves us, and we can rejoice in him, for ever.

Rachel Boulding

Disbelief and denial

Lord, let me know mine end, and the number of my days: that I may be certified how long I have to live. Behold, thou hast made my days as it were a span long: and mine age is even as nothing in respect of thee; and verily every man living is altogether vanity. For man walketh in a vain shadow, and disquieteth himself in vain: he heapeth up riches, and cannot tell who shall gather them. And now, Lord, what is my hope: truly my hope is even in thee.

'I can't believe this is happening.' A diagnosis of cancer—or any life-threatening disease—often seems inherently unbelievable. If I am the person who is ill, I cannot get my head round it, and nor can those around me. They struggle to make sense of what is being said and cannot believe that they have heard correctly.

Some people try to block it out—'This absolutely cannot be happening. I'm too young and I don't even feel unwell' or 'The doctors must be wrong: she looks fine and has a healthy lifestyle.' It seems as if something in human nature, especially in modern Western society, simply cannot grasp the idea of terminal illness as a personal experience. It might be an event in films or books, something that happens to other people, but not to me or those I love.

Why should it not happen to me, though? I know that people do die of diseases before they reach the average span of 80-something, so why not me? OK, I am not a smoker, and not obese, but all sorts of people get cancer.

When I was first diagnosed with secondary breast cancer—a return of the disease, which has now spread to various parts of my body—the idea of dying early played around in my head, coming round and back in a way that was like the experience of grief. Sometimes now, too, I can accept that it is happening, but often it seems like a bad dream from which I hope to wake.

Loving Father, draw me towards you and the truth of your complete knowledge of me. I exist in you, and my life is hidden in yours, however long it might be. Amen.

COLOSSIANS 3:1–4 (NRSV)

Processing the information

So if you have been raised with Christ, seek the things that are above, where Christ is, seated at the right hand of God. Set your minds on things that are above, not on things that are on earth, for you have died, and your life is hidden with Christ in God. When Christ who is your life is revealed, then you also will be revealed with him in glory.

Part of the process of facing up to life-threatening illness is the difficulty of absorbing a great deal of information in a relatively short time. Much of the news is technical—medical, even financial—and emotional. It would be hard to take in if I was studying it in an abstract sense or had time to take it all in, but the huge fact is that it is happening to me, right now.

There are so many different and new ideas that I do not understand, especially about treatments. I am neither a doctor nor a psychologist. It is just too much to take in, especially when I am not feeling 100% and am full of anxiety about the future. I cannot grasp what any of this might mean for me.

In some ways, this is an extension of the seemingly endless circles of denial that I wrote about yesterday. It is too complicated, so it cannot be happening. I think it is important not to pretend that this bafflement is anything but hard going and enduring. It will not be shaken off with a bright suggestion of 'You've got to be positive.' Yes, it can be offered up in prayer—this is something we can all try, even when we feel alone—and God understands pain, confusion and abandonment from the inside, having suffered on the cross.

None of this is going to be easy. We need to dig deep into our trust in God and our knowledge of his blessings. Then we might have a fuller sense of his grace, which will more thoroughly equip us to face the current confusion and look to the future with hope.

Heavenly Father, I cannot believe what is happening or take in what it means. Plant in me a mustard seed of faith in you, even in the deepest darkness, which may grow to a fuller understanding of your constant love for me. Amen.

Anger and envy—and trust

Trust in the Lord with all your heart, and do not rely on your own insight. In all your ways acknowledge him, and he will make straight your paths. Do not be wise in your own eyes; fear the Lord, and turn away from evil. It will be a healing for your flesh and a refreshment for your body.

The denial and dazed bewilderment of life-threatening illness never seem to go away completely, churning round in circles of variations on a theme, but other thoughts often sneak up on me, too. If I do not watch out, I find myself wondering what I have done to deserve this. The sense of 'Why not me?'—the knowledge that I have no more merit than anyone else, whether others are obese smokers or not—can get lost.

The fact is that illnesses happen in this world and can take anyone away before what they might think is their rightful span. Yes, we can contribute to our risk of dying, such as by binge drinking or driving dangerously, but mostly it is more a matter of 'Stuff happens.'

Still, I find myself looking enviously at the over-60s when I realise I will never see that decade for myself. People may be elderly and frail, but at least they are alive. There is another way of looking at this, too. Why are we all not more concerned about helping older people face death? Why should people feel so sorry for me and wonder how I am going to cope with dying in my 50s, when there are so many more people going through something similar in their later decades? Surely we should be doing much, much more to think about something that we all have to go through.

In a way (and I have to be careful how I put this, to avoid seeming to revel in the shock factor and goriness of it all), it is a privilege to have a chance to contemplate such matters with an earlier end in sight. It concentrates the mind and helps to undermine some of the inevitable denial, so that I can focus on what really counts.

Lord God of the universe, lead me into your ways and away from the twisted paths of self-righteousness and envy. Amen

ISAIAH 55:1–3 (NRSV, abridged)

In the context of God's grace

Ho, everyone who thirsts, come to the waters; and you that have no money, come, buy and eat!… Why do you spend your money for that which is not bread, and your labour for that which does not satisfy?… Incline your ear, and come to me; listen, so that you may live. I will make with you an everlasting covenant, my steadfast, sure love for David.

At such points of feeling battered by the maelstrom of emotions, fear, confusing information and bewilderment, it is easy to lose sight of what really matters and the true state of the universe. The fact is that God has created the world and each one of us, and we exist to love him and reflect his love to others. He invites every individual to share abundant life in him and it is up to us how we respond.

Whether I have decades of life ahead or only a few weeks, months or years, there are things I can do, right now, to say 'Yes' to what he offers and bask in the warmth of his grace. It is about making the most of what I have.

Yes, there is a time to grieve for a future I might not have and the loss of experiences I might be looking forward to, but there is so much that I can do now, whatever might happen. I can enjoy God's gifts, right here. As Denise Inge, the Christian scholar, wrote when she knew she was dying in her early 50s, 'The cancer has not made life more precious—that would make it seem like something fragile to lock away in the cupboard. No, it has made it more delicious' (*A Tour of Bones*, Continuum, 2014, p. 7).

This is not a case of pretending that the grief and anxiety have gone away; it is more a case of needing to realise they are not the whole picture. Sometimes, it is useful to remind myself of this, perhaps with deep breaths and words such as the Jesus Prayer: 'Lord Jesus Christ, Son of the living God, have mercy on me, a sinner.'

Loving Father, guide me to see beyond my immediate fears and to know that you are alongside me, whether or not I sense you. Amen

Psalm 139:1–6 (NRSV)

O LORD, you have searched me and known me. You know when I sit down and when I rise up; you discern my thoughts from far away. You search out my path and my lying down, and are acquainted with all my ways. Even before a word is on my tongue, O Lord, you know it completely. You hem me in, behind and before, and lay your hand upon me. Such knowledge is too wonderful for me; it is so high that I cannot attain it.

Most holy and eternal God, lord and sovereign of all the creatures, I humbly present to thy divine majesty, myself, my soul and body, my thoughts and my words, my actions and intentions, my passions and my sufferings, to be disposed by thee to thy glory; to be blessed by thy providence; to be guided by thy counsel; to be sanctified by thy Spirit; and afterwards that my body and soul may be received into glory; for nothing can perish which is under thy custody, and the enemy of souls cannot devour what is thy portion, nor take it out of thy hands. This day, O Lord, and all the days of my life, I dedicate to thy honour, and the actions of my calling to the uses of grace, and the religion of all my days to be united to the merits and intercession of my holy Saviour, Jesus; that, in him and for him, I may be pardoned and accepted.

Jeremy Taylor (1613–67)

In uncertainty: seek the Lord

Seek the Lord while he may be found, call upon him while he is near; let the wicked forsake their way, and the unrighteous their thoughts; let them return to the Lord, that he may have mercy on them, and to our God, for he will abundantly pardon. For my thoughts are not your thoughts, nor are your ways my ways, says the Lord.

Facing life-threatening illness is part of a delicate, often fragile balance, which constantly needs to be renegotiated. It is between, on the one hand, some sort of realism about the medical facts—the way that the cancer has spread in my body—and, on the other, the sense that I am not giving up and deciding to die. I trust in the Lord, live in hope and try to make the most of what I have. This can be true whether I might have only weeks to live and be in a frail state or I am feeling well and have years ahead.

Often, it is the uncertainty that seems most difficult. It can seem debilitating, making planning impossible, and even thinking about the future seems fraught with danger. If we all knew how long we had on this planet, we fantasise that we would know securely where we were; we would be able to map out the time ahead and everything would be fine and dandy, but this is only a dream. There are so many things we can never know and we had better get used to it.

So we can make the most of the opportunities we have and relish each day and moment of blessing. As Denise Inge wrote, 'Contemplating mortality is not about being prepared to die, it is about being prepared to live… Living isn't something outside you that you will do one day when you have organised your life a little better. It comes from deep in the centre of yourself. You have to let the life in, there at the deepest part, and live it from the inside out' (*A Tour of Bones*, Continuum, 2014, pp. 188–189).

'I believe in the sun, even when it doesn't shine. I believe in love, even when I don't feel it. I believe in God, even when he is silent.' (Written by German Jews suffering Nazi persecution)

When those fears come back

Hear my prayer, O Lord, and with thine ears consider my calling: hold not thy peace at my tears. For I am a stranger with thee: and a sojourner, as all my fathers were. O spare me a little, that I may recover my strength: before I go hence, and be no more seen.

As I said earlier, the idea of facing death feels a bit like going through bereavement: it involves stages of denial, anger, regret, depression and, if you are really blessed, occasional elements of acceptance. 'Stages' feels like a misleading term, though, because of the way these aspects of grief do not follow a linear order: they come, go, return and overlap, several of them at the same time.

Despite my endless desire to wriggle out of confronting the big issues, I think it would be healthy to tackle my real fears about dying as honestly as I can. Anything else feels like ducking my responsibilities and the tremendous opportunity that all this presents to explore the fundamental truths of the life God has given us.

Many people are obviously worried by the process of dying—the potential for physical pain and the isolation of going away alone. There is also the revolting unpleasantness of bodily functions, smells and the indignity of being unable to take care of myself. None of this is surprising, because it is part of our essential humanity and our wish to live decently and keep parts of our self and our body private.

Strangely, though, the physical aspects do not happen to worry me so much. End-of-life palliative care is excellent now where I live in Britain—thanks partly to the work of Christians such as Cecily Saunders, the founder of the hospice movement. Medical members of staff are experts in managing pain and making people's last days as comfortable as possible. I might be being naive and overly optimistic about this, but I do not see any point in creating anxiety where I feel none at the moment. No, my main source of worry is about those left behind, which I will come to tomorrow.

Loving Father, work in me: build me up to face my fears clearly and to trust in your steadfast love. Amen.

The grief of those left behind

The king was deeply moved, and went up to the chamber over the gate, and wept; and as he went, he said, 'O my son Absalom, my son, my son Absalom! Would that I had died instead of you, O Absalom, my son, my son!' It was told Joab, 'The king is weeping and mourning for Absalom.' So the victory that day was turned into mourning for all the troops; for the troops heard that day, 'The king is grieving for his son.'

My friends will be sad and will miss me, but my closest family will suffer most—just as I would if any of them were to die. My son, who is in his late teens, will grow up without me. If it all goes most unexpectedly well, I might just about last until he turns 20, but he will go through the rest of his life without a mother. My husband will lose me after three decades of marriage and there will be a gap by his side, even if he remarries (which I do hope he will, for all our sakes). Another hope is that my mother, now in her 90s, will die before me. She says she is working on it—bizarre though it is to put it like this. It will also be hard for my brothers. I know that if any of them died, I would feel as if I had had a limb amputated, as I have a deep, visceral sense of being someone with three big brothers. This is an essential part of me, which I can never change.

It is not that I am so wonderful as a wife, mother, daughter or sister; it is just that I am the one they are used to. This is me, with all my faults and blessings. If my experience with dead friends and family is anything to go by, they will miss the exasperating parts as much as the lovely ones. This does not seem fair on them and I only pray that they can turn to God and the love of others to find comfort and hope.

Loving Father, in their time of loneliness and grief, draw my family and friends to you and your grace. Help them to know your presence beside them. Amen.

Romans 8:35–39 (KJV)

WHO shall separate us from the love of Christ? shall tribulation, or distress, or persecution, or famine, or nakedness, or peril, or sword? As it is written, For thy sake we are killed all the day long; we are accounted as sheep for the slaughter. Nay, in all these things we are more than conquerors through him that loved us. For I am persuaded, that neither death, nor life, nor angels, nor principalities, nor powers, nor things present, nor things to come, Nor height, nor depth, nor any other creature, shall be able to separate us from the love of God, which is in Christ Jesus our Lord.

I am no longer my own, but yours. Put me to what you will, rank me with whom you will. Put me to doing, put me to suffering. Let me be employed for you or laid aside for you. Exalted for you or brought low for you. Let me be full, let me be empty. Let me have all things, let me have nothing. I freely and heartily yield all things to your pleasure and disposal. And now, O glorious and blessed God, Father, Son, and Holy Spirit, you are mine and I am yours. So be it. And the covenant which I have made on earth, let it be ratified in heaven. Amen.

Methodist Covenant Prayer

JOHN 11:33, 35–36, 43–44 (NRSV)

Do something—not nothing

When Jesus saw her [Mary] weeping, and the Jews who came with her also weeping, he was greatly disturbed in spirit and deeply moved… Jesus began to weep. So the Jews said, 'See how he loved him!'… He cried with a loud voice, 'Lazarus, come out!' The dead man came out.

Sometimes it can seem as if the worst part about being seriously ill is others' reactions. Suddenly, everyone treats you differently, and this can hurt. When people ask what they should say or do to help, I would suggest that the most important thing is to say or do *something* and not avoid the person who is ill. The most damaging approach you can take is to shut someone out. Much of this is similar to when someone has been bereaved.

Almost always, it is better to say anything, very briefly, rather than nothing at all. The paralysing fear of your saying the wrong or hurtful thing is as nothing compared to the other person's pain at being shunned. Many ill people will have heard it all before anyway and got used to ignoring unhelpful comments. So, well-wishers could start with a plain 'I'm sorry to hear…', carry on to 'Would it help for me to do X?' (where X is some specific task, such as a lift or practical help around the home) and perhaps end with 'I'll be thinking of you' or 'praying for you', depending on the person.

The idea of what is right for that person, at that moment, is crucial. Try to listen to them, without leaping in with your own comments. When they are talking about their condition, a simple 'Yes, I see' or 'That must have been hard' can be more helpful than 'That's like the time when I…'. It can also be useful to leave them an escape clause, such as 'Maybe that's not where you are right now.'

For myself, I find that assurances about medical advances, brave fights, a positive attitude, or 'You'll be fine' can be hard to hear, though I try not to resort to violence when people mention them. They mean well, but they cannot really know how I feel.

Father, work within me, so that I see others in the light of your grace; and have mercy on us all. Amen.

Yes, you would cope

But when that which is perfect is come, then that which is in part shall be done away… For now we see through a glass, darkly; but then face to face: now I know in part; but then shall I know even as also I am known. And now abideth faith, hope, charity, these three; but the greatest of these is charity.

When you are ill—or, indeed, going through any serious trauma—you can often sense that behind people's kind enquiries about how you are coping is a huge, unspoken fear: 'How would I deal with that?' swiftly followed by 'I'd probably crumble completely.'

I'd want to say: 'No, you wouldn't crack up: most people don't.' They just get on with the medical stuff, turning up and being borne along the conveyor belt of appointments. Behind the brave face there might be moments of terror or sheer weariness: quiet tears in the bathroom, bleak times in a sleepless night, and odd catches of 'What on earth am I going to do?', at the most inconvenient time, just as you're filling the kettle. But mostly, you muddle along, managing it all without fuss or emotional scenes.

The thing is that you never, ever, really know. In extreme situations, doctors might tell you that you've got months, or even weeks, to live; but actually, mostly they just try different treatments, or send you for further tests—until you don't really know what is happening. Even if you are given a short time left, you usually don't know exactly when you're going to die, until the very end. So you end up living in great uncertainty. And this drags on.

If you are positive about it, you try to make the most of what you have. But this is also when we all—those who are ill and those around them—need to look to God's love, the charity that abideth above all, as this passage puts it, and realise that all this uncertainty will come to an end. We will be taken up in God. He knows each one of us, better than we know ourselves, in all our anxieties and nameless dread. And we are secure in him, in every part of ourselves known by him.

Take a few moments to ponder what it means that God knows you thoroughly, and still cherishes you.

Psalm 139:9–12 (KJV)

God in the dark

If I take the wings of the morning, and dwell in the uttermost parts of the sea; Even there shall thy hand lead me, and thy right hand shall hold me. If I say, Surely the darkness shall cover me; even the night shall be light about me. Yea, the darkness hideth not from thee; but the night shineth as the day: the darkness and the light are both alike to thee.

Many of my kind friends are also perhaps wondering: 'What does it really feel like, when you know you're going to die soon?' They might wonder how I can go about my everyday life, when it's all going to be taken away. The simple answer is that it doesn't really feel like that. At some level, you don't really believe that it is going to happen. When you try to dig more deeply, you still struggle to take it in. One hospital chaplain reassured me that you're not *supposed* to get your head around it; most of us lack the capacity to cope with such information.

So perhaps this is when you relish what you have: seeing friends and family, and perhaps visiting places you've always wanted to go. And this can be joyful, as you cherish those times, and live in the happiness of the moment.

But then, you've ticked off the bucket list (if you like that sort of thing, which I don't), settled your affairs as much as you can, and er… you're still here—diminishing physically, but keeping breathing. This is surely the position of many people in their 80s, 90s and beyond: not as fit as they once were, but still with us. This is the very point, the boring stage, where we need most help. It is when habits of prayer, serious reading, and worship matter more: they can carry us through the dull slog, when we don't know what is really happening and don't know how long it will last.

There might be more darkness to endure, but this is when we need to realise that God is still there, cherishing us. This will not look like an abyss to God, for 'the darkness and the light are both alike to thee'.

Heavenly Father, guide me with your light in the darkness. Amen

Dependent on God

When Jesus saw his mother and the disciple whom he loved standing beside her, he said to his mother, 'Woman, here is your son.' Then he said to the disciple, 'Here is your mother.' And from that hour the disciple took her into his own home.

One of the aspects of being ill that can be hard to cope with—and which applies to many serious illnesses—is the business of becoming dependent and having to accept help. Many of us dread the thought of being a burden. After a lifetime of being the one who takes action and helps others, it goes against the grain when the positions are reversed and we cannot do basic tasks ourselves. It robs us of our purpose and our sense of who we are. It is a loss of control that can hurt as much as the illness or its treatment.

This anxiety is definitely not the preserve of icy perfectionists or manic control-freaks: some fear the loss of dignity that turns them from an autonomous human into an anonymous object for medics; others shrivel at the thought of no longer being able to provide for their families. It can be awkward to ask for help, even when we're in real need. I remember the waves of gratitude to the friend who kicked off the embarrassing process of drawing up a rota of lifts to drive me to radiotherapy. She approached people fearlessly, in the way that is easier to do if the help is for someone else.

The best way I found through this minefield was for the helpers to be as specific as possible about what they could offer (tasks such as laundry, cleaning or cooking are often useful). Being the one who was ministered to, I made myself imagine what it would be like if the tables were turned: if my friend was ill, of course I would volunteer to help.

We can only remind ourselves of our place as God's children, under his care. We are all dependent on him, and attempts at asserting our little selves can be merely fierce petty pieces of pride.

'Truly I tell you, unless you change and become like children, you will never enter the kingdom of heaven. Whoever becomes humble like this child is the greatest in the kingdom of heaven' (Matthew 18:3–4, NRSV).

Psalm 42:1–3, 7–8 (NRSV)

As a deer longs for flowing streams, so my soul longs for you, O God. My soul thirsts for God, for the living God. When shall I come and behold the face of God? My tears have been my food day and night, while people say to me continually, 'Where is your God?'… Deep calls to deep at the thunder of your cataracts; all your waves and your billows have gone over me. By day the LORD commands his steadfast love, and at night his song is with me, a prayer to the God of my life.

Almighty God, by whose mercy my life has been yet prolonged to another year, grant that thy mercy may not be in vain. Let not my years be multiplied to increase my guilt, but as age advances, let me become more pure in my thoughts, more regular in my desires, and more obedient to thy laws. Let not the cares of the world distract me, nor the evils of age overwhelm me. But continue and increase thy lovingkindness towards me, and when thou shalt call me hence, receive me to everlasting happiness, for the sake of Jesus Christ, our Lord. Amen.

Samuel Johnson (1709–84)

Resources for hope

Praised be the Lord daily: even the God who helpeth us, and poureth his benefits upon us. He is our God, even the God of whom cometh salvation: God is the Lord, by whom we escape death… Thy God hath sent forth strength for thee: stablish the thing, O God, that thou hast wrought in us.

In the midst of these inner conflicts, God continues to pour out his blessings on us. He offers a huge range of resources that can help us personally. Part of this is evident in the Christian tradition of a 'good death'. The idea may have gone out of fashion, partly due to our modern reluctance to face the ultimate reality and our over-reliance on medical advances to solve our problems, but the help is there. So we can turn to the example of Christians such as John Donne (1572–1631), the poet whose passionate sexual writing developed into equally passionate words of desire for God (see *New Daylight: January– April 2014* for notes I wrote about him).

Donne was praised by the people of his time for having fashioned a good death. This involved practical activities, public and private, including making a careful will and inviting his friends to say goodbye. He also commissioned a sculpture of himself for his grave, which is still in St Paul's Cathedral to this day.

It might seem overly morbid, but I love the bracing realism of the way he posed for an artist to draw him as a shrouded corpse for his tomb. He seemed to want to confront what his dead body would look like. Perhaps such a literal depiction helped to bring home to him what his own death would be like; then it could hold fewer terrors. It is the unknown that frightens us most. Having the chance to create a true-to-death image must have felt like a good opportunity to do this.

In his final sermon, known as 'Death's Duel', he began with the words above from Psalm 68: 'He is our God…'. His message was that the whole of life looks forward to the end: 'all our periods and transitions in this life are so many passages from death to death'.

Father, ground me in your strength and grace, right to the end. Amen

LUKE 23:36–37, 46–47 (NRSV)

Looking to Jesus on the cross

The soldiers also mocked him, coming up and offering him sour wine, and saying, 'If you are the King of the Jews, save yourself!'… Then Jesus, crying with a loud voice, said, 'Father, into your hands I commend my spirit.' Having said this, he breathed his last. When the centurion saw what had taken place, he praised God and said, 'Certainly this man was innocent.'

As we read yesterday, John Donne's approach, revelling in the details of death, is a huge contrast to modern attitudes. Instead of seeing death as part of life, we now regard it as a weird, infinitely postponeable and unconnected horror in the distant future. Why can we not grasp that it is perfectly natural and will happen to us all? Who are we trying to kid? Fool ourselves we do, though, and modern Western society seems to encourage us to do so. We hide death away in hospitals and shield our children from it, so that it no longer seems like a normal part of life. This can foster only fear of its unfamiliarity and mystery.

Christians used to be encouraged to look specifically at Jesus' death as an example, drawing on the fact of his saving sacrifice to find positive aspects to the end of life, as well as looking to his approach to the process of his death. So, just as he did not flinch from death—despite the genuine fear he expressed in Gethsemane—and later gave up his spirit to his Father in a positive way, so Christians are spurred on to face their end squarely and to be mindful of it.

Sometimes the idea of meeting death eagerly and seeing it as a spiritual opportunity could veer towards the obsessive, but, at its best, it fostered a healthy honesty. The Gospels' descriptions of Jesus' sufferings also gave an immediate well of experience that Christians could draw on. They could set their own pain alongside his, secure in the knowledge that he had endured worse horrors, both physical and in terms of his abandonment by so many of those he loved.

Lord Jesus, you died to set me free from the terrors of death. Show me how to set my sufferings at the foot of your cross. Amen.

Torn between grief and hope

For since death came through a man, the resurrection of the dead comes also through a man. For as in Adam all die, so in Christ all will be made alive. But each in turn: Christ, the firstfruits; then, when he comes, those who belong to him. Then the end will come, when he hands over the kingdom to God the Father after he has destroyed all dominion, authority and power. For he must reign until he has put all his enemies under his feet. The last enemy to be destroyed is death.

Most vitally, Jesus has defeated death. He lives now and will raise us with him. Christians should never minimise or dismiss the suffering of death and the shattering grief it causes, yet our pain is mingled with hope. The frightening separation of the dead person from their earlier existence and those left behind when the one they had loved is taken from them is set alongside a wider picture (see 1 Corinthians 15:54–57, the reading a couple of pages ahead). It can be hard to sense it, but even if it is only faintly in the background, it is something we can grow to appreciate, even if this takes a long time.

Of course, a death usually feels like searing pain, a terrible ripping apart of the normal order of life—even if the person dying is full of years, after a contented life, and a fine Christian. We will still miss that person terribly.

Shakespeare offers a lighthearted-but-serious version of this sense of being torn in *Twelfth Night* (Act 1, Scene 5), when Feste, the clown or 'Fool', tries to jolt Olivia out of her sadness, as she has been mired too long in grief for her brother. He declares, 'I think his soul is in hell' to provoke her reaction. She says, 'I know his soul is in heaven, fool.' He replies, 'The more fool, madonna, to mourn for your brother's soul being in heaven.'

Loving Father, guide me through the mixture of hopes and fears as I look forward to the coming of your kingdom. Amen.

PSALM 90:4–5, 10, 12 (BCP)

Realism in the face of the end

For a thousand years in thy sight are but as yesterday: seeing that is past as a watch in the night. As soon as thou scatterest them they are even as a sleep: and fade away suddenly like the grass… The days of our age are threescore years and ten; and though men be so strong that they come to fourscore years: yet is their strength then but labour and sorrow; so soon passeth it away, and we are gone… So teach us to number our days: that we may apply our hearts unto wisdom.

Another positive aspect of dying that we have lost is its public nature. In many places in earlier centuries, the deathbed was a busy place, with streams of visitors. People could say their goodbyes simply, familiar as they were with the process. Hospices do their best to support those who are dying, both on their premises and in people's own homes, but often this is a struggle against the prevailing culture of the medicalisation of death and the desire to separate it from natural human interaction.

Despite this, we still rightly praise those who speak publicly about death—such as the actor Lynda Bellingham, who was frank in 2014 about stopping her gruelling cancer treatment. She realised that prolonging it would give her only a little longer and that time would be ravaged by sickness, so she decided to go for quality rather than quantity and died soon afterwards. She was applauded by the Marie Curie charity for the benefit she brought to others by using 'the language of acceptance' so openly.

Obviously, different people are on different paths at various stages, but we really need to face up to the fact that there can come a point at which there is not much more that the doctors or we can do to keep us alive for much longer. As Lynda Bellingham said about stopping treatment, 'This is my way of taking back control. I'm not giving up, just being realistic.' At this stage, it can be better for everyone for the patient to spend their last days with family and friends, saying goodbye and preparing spiritually.

Father, prepare me for the wonders of your nearer love. Amen.

1 John 3:1–2 (NRSV)

SEE what love the Father has given us, that we should be called children of God; and that is what we are. The reason the world does not know us is that it did not know him. Beloved, we are God's children now; what we will be has not yet been revealed. What we do know is this: when he is revealed, we will be like him, for we will see him as he is.

Bring us, O Lord God, at our last awakening
into the house and gate of heaven,
to enter into that gate and dwell in that house,
where there shall be no darkness nor dazzling, but one equal light;
no noise nor silence, but one equal music;
no fears nor hopes, but one equal possession;
no ends nor beginnings, but one equal eternity;
in the habitations of thy glory and dominion,
world without end. Amen.

Eric Milner-White (1884–1963), using phrases from a sermon by John Donne (1572–1631)

Between realism and positivity

When this perishable body puts on imperishability, and this mortal body puts on immortality, then the saying that is written will be fulfilled: 'Death has been swallowed up in victory.' 'Where, O death, is your victory? Where, O death, is your sting?' The sting of death is sin, and the power of sin is the law. But thanks be to God, who gives us the victory through our Lord Jesus Christ.

The most senior cancer doctor I have spoken to assured me that the most important factor in medical treatment is the patient's attitude. Some people can drive themselves towards death, but others carry on much longer if they have something or someone to live for. People of faith do fare better. Reliable research backs up the fact that religious believers really do last longer with life-limiting illnesses.

There is another side to all this, however. I can try to stay strong and summon up a sunny outlook, particularly if it helps those around me, yet I have to admit that I need to be realistic: I will die before too long. It is a balancing act between genuine hope and the need to find the positives on the one hand and, on the other, a true assessment of my medical condition.

It can sometimes strike a false note to say, 'I'm going to fight this' if disease has advanced so far in my body. Eventually, it will become a battle I can never win. What is more, couching it in these military terms can even make it feel like my fault for not trying hard enough—as if I am dying because I have failed to make enough effort. Being honest, though, I can say, 'I'm going to face this head on.' I can engage with the medical details and try to make my last days count.

There are positive steps that most of us can take. We can assure our family and friends of our love, thank people who have helped us, phone or write to others (one line on a card can be enough) and make our peace with God. Hospice staff members often report how patients have found resolution and fulfilment by taking such actions.

'My grace is sufficient for you, for power is made perfect in weakness' (2 Corinthians 12:9, NRSV).

He shall be our guide unto death

Great is the Lord, and highly to be praised: in the city of our God, even upon his holy hill… God is well known in her palaces as a sure refuge… We wait for thy loving-kindness, O God: in the midst of thy temple… For this God is our God for ever and ever: he shall be our guide unto death.

Whether we are dying ourselves or bracing ourselves for the death of someone close to us, we can at least try to take some of the fear out of the process of departing. Ignorance and the perfectly understandable reluctance to face the painful realities make it all harder, but it is the ill-defined terrors that conjure up much worse horrors and strike dread into our hearts.

So we could try to begin talking to those around us about the stages or various aspects of dying, death and grief. These may be the most difficult conversations we will ever face, but it is surely worth attempting. There might well come times when all this is too much of a burden and we are too ill to cope with it, but we could mention the love and faith that will not let us go, whatever losses engulf us. Without trying to present ourselves as in some way saintly, it helps to be as specific as we can about exactly what does and does not frighten us and in what ways our beliefs equip us to confront what lies ahead. If we can get this out into the open, it cannot but help those near to us, and us, too.

So I have tried in a small way to reassure my family and best friends that I am not afraid of the process of dying, but am churned up by the prospect of leaving them. Often, widows and widowers feel they need some kind of permission to remarry, so, in an attempt to head off any false honouring of our memories, we can also encourage our families to enjoy life and meet new people after we have gone.

God, our loving Father, prepare me to face my death honestly, and work with your comfort within those who will be left behind. Amen.

1 JOHN 4:16b–19 (NRSV)

Perfect love casts out fear

God is love, and those who abide in love abide in God, and God abides in them. Love has been perfected among us in this: that we may have boldness on the day of judgement, because as he is, so are we in this world. There is no fear in love, but perfect love casts out fear; for fear has to do with punishment, and whoever fears has not reached perfection in love. We love because he first loved us.

Before I was told that this cancer was terminal, I had no idea how much people were afraid of death. The more I talked about it with various people, the more I realised how many of us nurse a numbing dread of both the process of dying and death itself. Sometimes I want to argue this out, but I doubt this would work: we all cherish our secret fears, and often you have to know people very well to be able to challenge them.

Some Christians find comfort in speculating on the details of the next life, pondering on what heaven might be like. Fair enough, if that strengthens their faith—though it does not do much for me. This might be a failure of my imagination, but I don't believe we can ever know what awaits us: it is beyond me, in more than one sense. And yet I do have a strong sense that we will be with God, in some way that I cannot grasp now.

What I also know is that God has reached out to us. He first loved us (v. 19), and gave us the capability to love him, as well as those around us, and ourselves. Is he wrong to love me? It is not pride to say: 'No, I hope not.' This passage tells us 'that we may have boldness on the day of judgement' (v. 17), so we should try to get used to the idea. Yes, it can be puffed up into selfishness, but God still loves us and lives in us (v. 16). This is the love that drives out all fear. We can be open to its work within us, now and in the life to come.

Heavenly Father, work within me, in your lovingkindness, to drive out my fears. Amen

Revelation 21:1–4 (NRSV)

THEN I saw a new heaven and a new earth; for the first heaven and the first earth had passed away, and the sea was no more. And I saw the holy city, the new Jerusalem, coming down out of heaven from God, prepared as a bride adorned for her husband. And I heard a loud voice from the throne saying, 'See, the home of God is among mortals. He will dwell with them as their God; they will be his peoples, and God himself will be with them; he will wipe every tear from their eyes. Death will be no more; mourning and crying and pain will be no more, for the first things have passed away.'

How fresh, O Lord, how sweet and clean
Are thy returns! ev'n as the flowers in spring…
Grief melts away
Like snow in May,
As if there were no such cold thing…

Who would have thought my shrivelled heart
Could have recovered greenness? It was gone
Quite underground…

These are thy wonders, Lord of love,
To make us see we are but flowers that glide;
Which when we once can find and prove,
Thou hast a garden for us, where to bide.

From 'The Flower' by George Herbert (1593–1633)

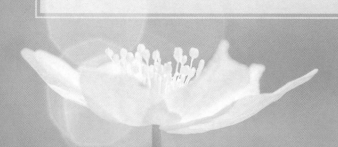

Where to go for help

The most obvious place to get help is from your own minister or priest. Every pastor will have had some training and experience of helping people to die well, and I have found that some of the most unlikely-seeming ones can tap into a wealth of wisdom. Of course, many lay Christians have particular gifts in this area, too.

There are also hospital and hospice chaplains, who are great specialists, even if they might not know you as an individual as thoroughly as your own minister (though such unfamiliarity can have its advantages, too). I have found it tremendously liberating to talk to clergy who are not at all alarmed about discussing death openly.

Hospices are wonderful powerhouses of care—full of joy and relish for life, which offer counselling, spiritual ministry, friendship, information, and much more. I have been shocked, though, by how many people are afraid of going near them, mistakenly associating them only with the last gasps of grim death.

Many charities provide great resources, too, including discussion groups on the Internet and in different parts of the country, publications full of information and personal stories, support on the phone, and experts to consult. For example, Macmillan Cancer Care offers masses of help, including a booklet, *End of Life: A guide*, produced jointly with Marie Curie, which itself offers a huge range of services for dying people (www.macmillan.org.uk; www.mariecurie.org.uk). Similarly, Penny Brohn UK runs an online community, as well as courses which incorporate spirituality in its whole-person approach (www.pennybrohn.org.uk). Facebook hosts groups related to many different conditions, including heart disease and stroke, for people to contact others (www.facebook.com), and there are vast numbers of blogs, reflecting various experiences.

Dying Matters is a coalition of organisations dedicated to discussing death more openly and planning for the end of life (www.dyingmatters.org.uk). There is also a growing literature of modern testimony about what it is like to face death—much of it with some element of general spirituality rather than being specifically Christian. I have relished books such as *Late Fragments* by Kate Gross (Collins, 2015) and *Being Mortal* by Atul Gawande (Profile, 2015). Then there are Christian resources, such as *The Enduring Melody* by Michael Mayne (DLT, 2006) and *Our Last Awakening: Poems for living in the face of death* by Janet Morley (SPCK, 2016), as well as historical classics such as *Holy Dying* by Jeremy Taylor and much of the work of John Donne. Others have recommended *Living With Dying* by Grace Sheppard (DLT, 2010) and *Heaven's Morning* by David Winter (BRF, 2016).

Also from The Bible Reading Fellowship

Ill Health
Wendy Bray
978 0 85746 231 2 £3.99

Bereavement
Jean Watson
978 0 85746 326 5 £3.99

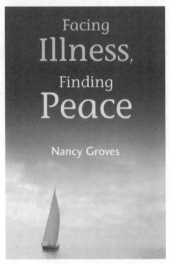

Facing Illness, Finding Peace
Nancy Groves
978 0 85746 242 8 £6.99

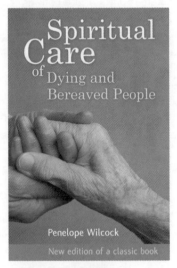

Spiritual Care of Dying and Bereaved People
Penelope Wilcock
978 0 85746 115 5 £9.99

brfonline.org.uk